NOBODY LIKES A C*CKBLOCK

R. SWANSON

ILLUSTRATED BY JESS JANSEN

NOBODY LIKES A C*CKBLOCK

Copyright 2016©Osun Books
All rights reserved.

R.Swanson[Writer],Jess Jansen[Illustrator]

ISBN: 978-0-692-63675-6

The stars are out,
it's dark outside.

I can see that there's **sleep**
inside of your eyes.

stay warm in your bed,
on our door **do not knock**.

Because **nobody** likes
a cockblock.

Daddy worked all day long.
He's tired and lonely.

There's a **small,small,small chance** that your mother might blow me.

If you cry, no one's coming.
This may come as a shock,

but **nobody** likes
a cockblock.

I love mommy **so much.**
she's my favorite cutie

and tonight,
I would like a **Piece of that bootie.**

Don't ask for milk
or help with your socks

because **nobody** likes a cockblock.

The train's leaving the station,
it's about to go down.

My ticket is stamped
for a trip to **Pound Town.**

Your job is to sleep
like the heaviest rock.

Darling, **nobody** likes a cockblock.

Dinner was yummy.
For dessert you had fruit,

so don't say you're hungry
when we're knocking boots.

Your antics are like a knife
to my jock

and nobody likes a cockblock.

It's **not cool** to wait for us to get busy

to cry for a hug or go into a tizzy.

If our door is closed,
away you must walk

because
nobody likes a cockblock.

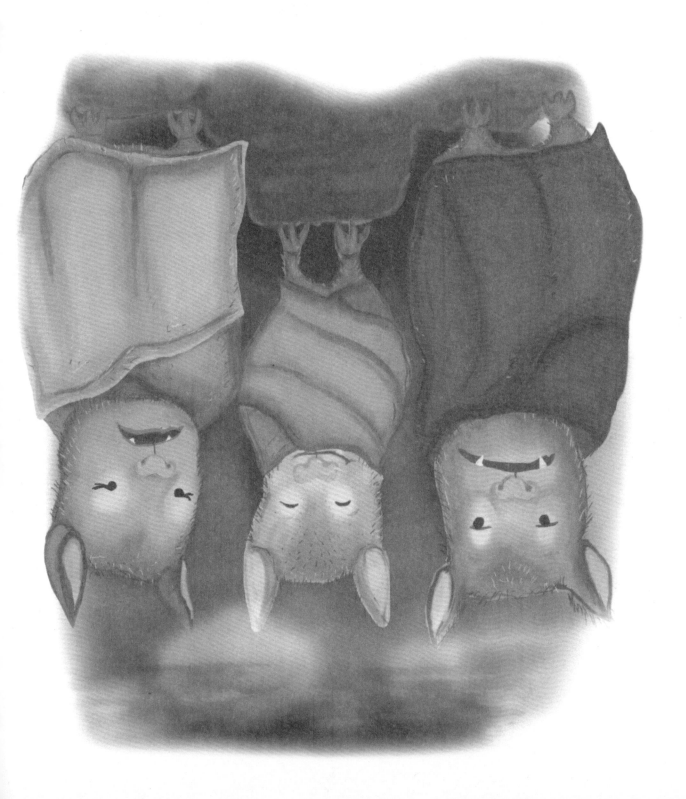

Curl up in your blanket.
Hug teddy so tight.

It's now time for daddy
to turn off the light.

Would you look at the time? It's **poontang o'clock!**

And **nobody** likes a cockblock.

Ok, one **last kiss.**
One **very fast** hug.

You're tucked in just right
like a **bug in a rug.**

We love you **so much** but **remember** this talk

and that **nobody likes a cockblock!**

The End

CPSIA information can be obtained
at www.ICGtesting.com
Printed in the USA
LVHW07n1616140818
586954LV00009B/103/P